CONTENTS

These adorable pillow friends are loved by kids and adults alike! They serve as both stuffed animal and comfy headrest in one. The square and round doggie face pillows work great as travel pillows because of their small size, and the jellybean and log pillows are wonderful for decorating the house or enticing you into a cozy nap. All of the pillows are simple to create and are made with easy-to-use and fluffy fabrics for the ultimate fuzzy friend!

JELLYBEAN PILLOW

This adorable project transforms your favorite dog into the shape of a jellybean. It is similar to a neck pillow, but in the form of your best canine friend. This project works well with plush fabrics like fleece, faux fur, or minky. The main difficulty can come from keeping track of all the small ear, tail, and foot pieces. Be sure not to skip the basting step and you'll tackle this project just fine.

The pattern comes with guides to make a Husky, Welsh Corgi, or Dalmatian, but the markings can be mixed, matched, or color-swapped to emulate your favorite furry pal! The patterns are made for fabric that is 60" (1525mm) wide, the common width for fleece and minky.

MATERIALS

- **For Husky:** ⅓ yd. (⅓m) gray plush fabric, ⅓ yd. (⅓m) white plush fabric
- **For Welsh Corgi:** ⅓ yd. (⅓m) white plush fabric, ½ yd. (⅓m) brown plush fabric
- **For Dalmatian:** ½ yd. (½m) white plush fabric, ¼ yd. (¼m) black plush fabric (for spots)
- Fabric for appliqué
- Batting
- Thread to match appliqué
- Thread to match plush fabrics
- Fusible web
- Stabilizer

TOOLS

- Fabric marker
- Fabric scissors
- Fabric pins
- Hand-sewing needle

How to Make the Jellybean Pillow

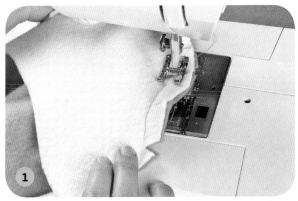

Sew the top to the bottom. Cut the pattern pieces from your fabric and make all applicable markings. Apply fusible web to the appliqué pieces. Sew the top pieces of the body to the bottom pieces for the respective front and back. Clip corners and curves and iron lightly.

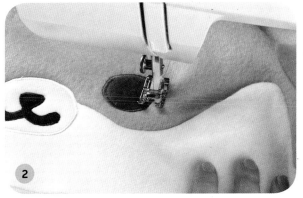

Appliqué. Iron the appliqué pieces to the front of the pillow following the pattern guidelines. Sew along the edges of the fabric.

Sew the ears, tails, and feet. Sew the ear, tail, and foot pieces together along the edges, leaving straight edges open for turning inside out. Turn the pieces inside out and stuff the feet lightly.

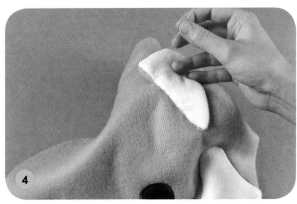

Sew the right ear to the face. Turn under edges of right ear and hand sew to the front as indicated by the pattern. Sew the back of the ear. [For Dalmatian: Fold the ears down and iron strongly to crease them.] Flip the front body piece over, and hand sew the ear to the face to keep it from flopping down.

Baste the ear, tail, and feet. Baste the ear, tail, and foot pieces to the edges of the front body piece as indicated by the pattern.

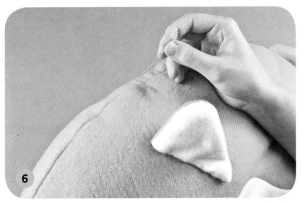

Sew the body. Sew the front to the back, creating the body of the pillow. Be sure to leave an opening as indicated by the pattern. Turn right side out and stuff semi-firmly, still keeping the shape flat. Hand sew the opening closed.

LOG PILLOW

You might be surprised how comfortable it is to sleep on something so simple. Make this pillow with minky and you're in for a real treat! Other knit plush fabrics, such as fleece and faux fur, can work for this project as well. The only challenge in this project may come from going around the curves on each end of the log. If you line up your markings correctly and stretch the fabric lightly to make it around the curves, you will have no problem. The patterns provide guides to make a Pig, Fox, and Kitty pillow. They are for 60" (1525mm)-wide fabric, the typical width for fleece and minky.

MATERIALS

- ½ yd. (½m) plush fabric
- For Fox: ⅛ yd. (⅛m) contrast plush fabric for ear tips
- Fabric for appliqué
- Batting
- Thread to match plush fabric
- Thread to match appliqué fabric
- Fusible web
- Stabilizer

TOOLS

- Fabric marker
- Fabric scissors
- Fabric pins
- Hand-sewing needle

How to Make the Log Pillow

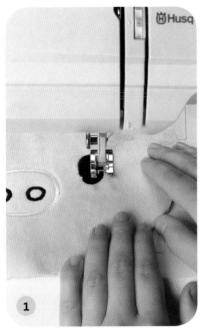

Appliqué. Cut the pattern pieces from your fabric and make all applicable markings. Apply fusible web to the appliqué pieces. Iron the appliqué pieces to the front of the pillow, following the pattern guidelines. Sew along the edges of the fabric and along any lines as indicated.

Sew the ears. [For Fox: Sew the ear base to the ear tip and finger press flat.] Sew the ear pieces together, leaving the bottom edge open. Turn them right side out.

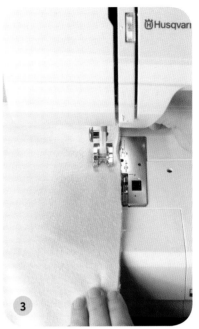

Sew the body. Sew the pillow body across the long seam, leaving an opening, as the pattern indicates, for turning the pillow right side out. Also, leave the two ends of the body open.

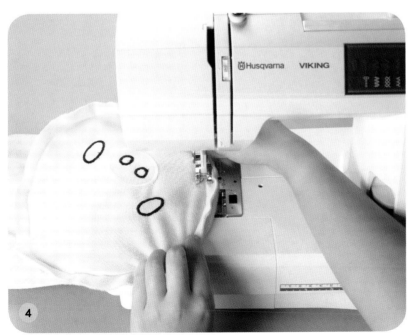

Sew the front and back. Sew the front and back circles to each end of the body, including ears where indicated by the pattern. Use the markings from the pattern to match up the center top and bottom of the face.

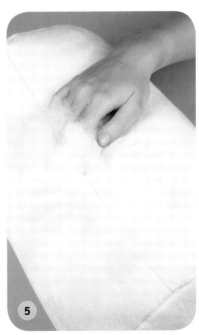

Finish. Turn the pillow right side out, stuff it firmly, and hand sew the opening closed.

SQUARE PILLOW

This project is another very simple shape that can be customized easily into all sorts of characters. The small and flat shape makes it a great travel or throw pillow. A knit plush fabric, such as fleece, minky, or faux fur, works best for this project. The challenge will come if you attempt the Squid, which calls for some tricky pivoting with corners. Take full advantage of the stretchy quality of fleece to make this work. Also, consider rounding your corners if necessary to make the process easier. The patterns provide guides to make a Squid, Raccoon, and Bear pillow. They are for 60" (1525mm)-wide fabric.

MATERIALS

- **For Squid:** ¾ yd. (¾m) plush fabric
- **For Bear:** ½ yd. (½m) plush fabric
- **For Raccoon:** ½ yd. (½m) plush fabric, ⅛ yd. (⅛m) contrasting fabric
- Fabric for appliqué
- Batting
- Fusible web
- Stabilizer
- Thread to match main plush fabric
- Thread to match contrasting fabric
- Thread to match appliqué fabric

TOOLS

- Fabric marker
- Fabric scissors
- Fabric pins
- Hand-sewing needle

ROUND PILLOW

This sweet project is very similar in construction to the Square Pillow. A knit plush fabric like fleece, minky, or faux fur works best for this project. The Husky pillow calls for some pivoting—don't be afraid to stretch your fleece to make everything line up. Also, remember you can round the corners if needed to make the process easier. The patterns provide guides to make a Husky, Welsh Corgi, and Dalmatian face pillow. Switch colors and markings to capture your favorite puppy in pillow form! The patterns are for 60" (1525mm)-wide fabric, the typical width for fleece and minky.

MATERIALS

- **For Husky:** ⅓ yd. (⅓m) white plush fabric, ⅔ yd. (⅔m) gray plush fabric
- **For Welsh Corgi:** ½ yd. (½m) brown plush fabric, ⅛ yd. (⅛m) white plush fabric
- **For Dalmatian:** ½ yd. (½m) white plush fabric, ¼ yd. (¼m) black plush fabric (for spots)
- Fabric for appliqué
- Batting
- Fusible web
- Stabilizer
- Thread to match appliqué fabric
- Thread to match plush fabrics

TOOLS

- Fabric marker
- Fabric scissors
- Fabric pins
- Hand-sewing needle

How to Make the Square and Round Pillow

1

For Husky: Sew front pieces. Sew the top front piece to the bottom front piece, pivoting at the corners.

2

Appliqué. Cut the pattern pieces from your fabric and make all applicable markings. Apply fusible web to the appliqué pieces. Iron the appliqué pieces to the main fabric following the pattern guidelines. Sew along the edges of the fabric.

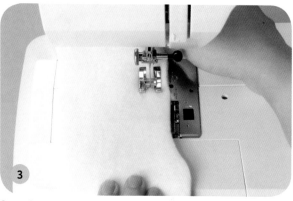

3

Sew the arms, ears, tentacles, and hood. Sew any arm and ear [For Squid: tentacle and hood] pieces together, leaving the straight edges open. Turn them right side out.

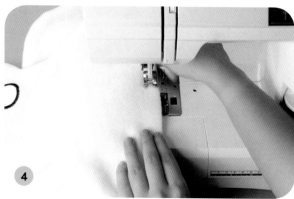

4

For Squid: Baste the hood. Pin the straight edges of the Squid hood around the top of the pillow front, matching the corners together. Clip the seam allowances in the hood to help it reach all the way around. Use a basting stitch to hold it in place for the next step. If you get puckers while doing this, try rounding the corners instead for an easier transition.

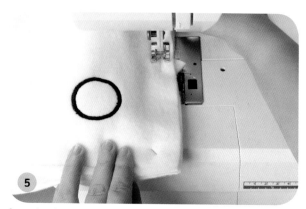

5

Sew the front to the back. Pin the front of the pillow to the back, inserting all arms, ears, and tentacles as indicated by the pattern. Sew them all in place, leaving an opening as indicated for turning it right side out.

6

Finish. Turn the pillow right side out, stuff it firmly, and hand sew the opening closed.

PATTERNS

Jellybean Pillow Patterns

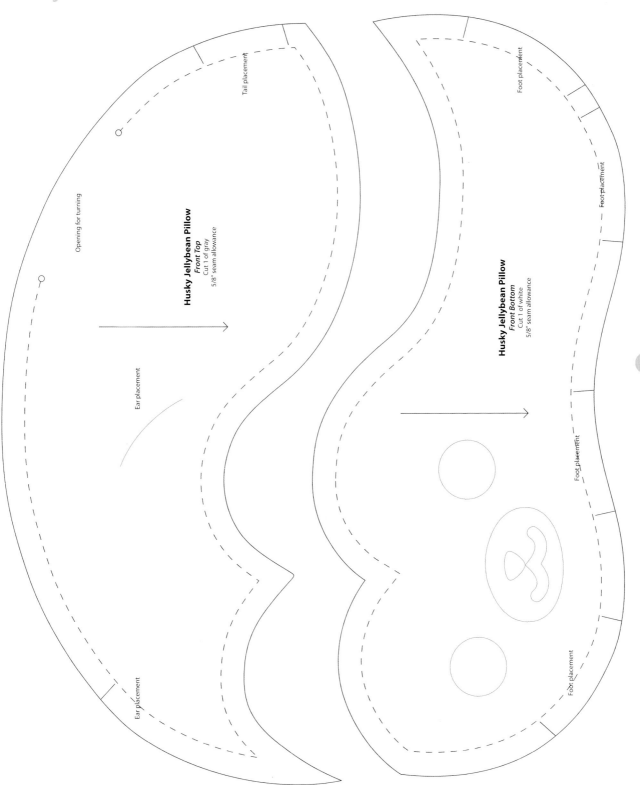

Husky Jellybean Pillow
Front Top
Cut 1 of gray
5/8" seam allowance

Opening for turning

Tail placement

Ear placement

Ear placement

Husky Jellybean Pillow
Front Bottom
Cut 1 of white
5/8" seam allowance

Foot placement

Foot placement

Foot placement

Foot placement

Foot placement

Enlarge pattern 250% for actual size.

PATTERNS

PET PILLOWS

12

Tail placement

Opening for turning

Welsh Corgi Jellybean Pillow
Top
Cut 2 of brown
5/8" seam allowance

Ear placement

Ear placement

Foot placement

Foot placement

Welsh Corgi Jellybean Pillow
Bottom
Cut 2 of white
5/8" seam allowance

Foot placement

Foot placement

Foot placement

Welsh Corgi Jellybean Pillow
Tail
Cut 2 of brown
5/8" seam allowance

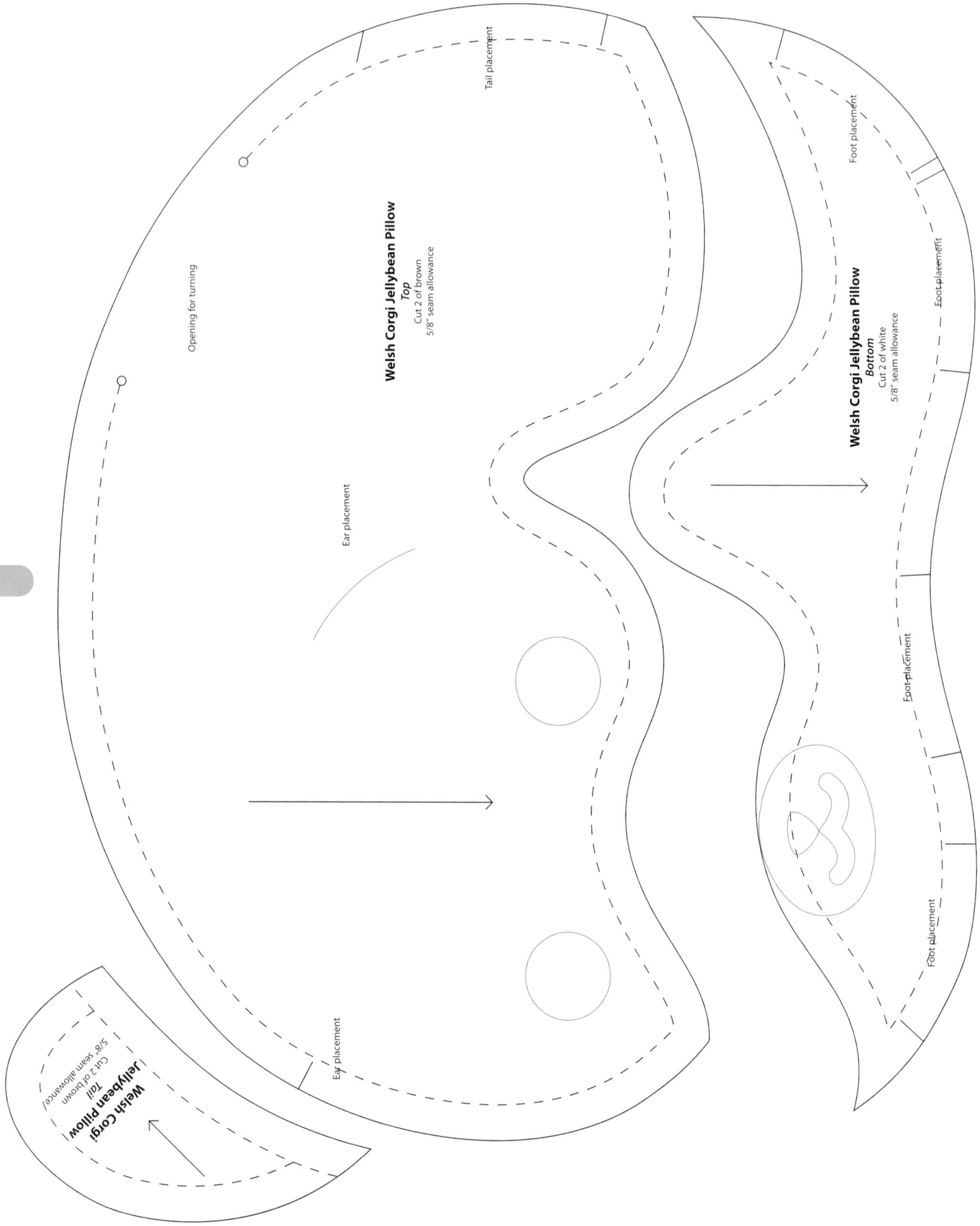

Enlarge pattern 250% for actual size.

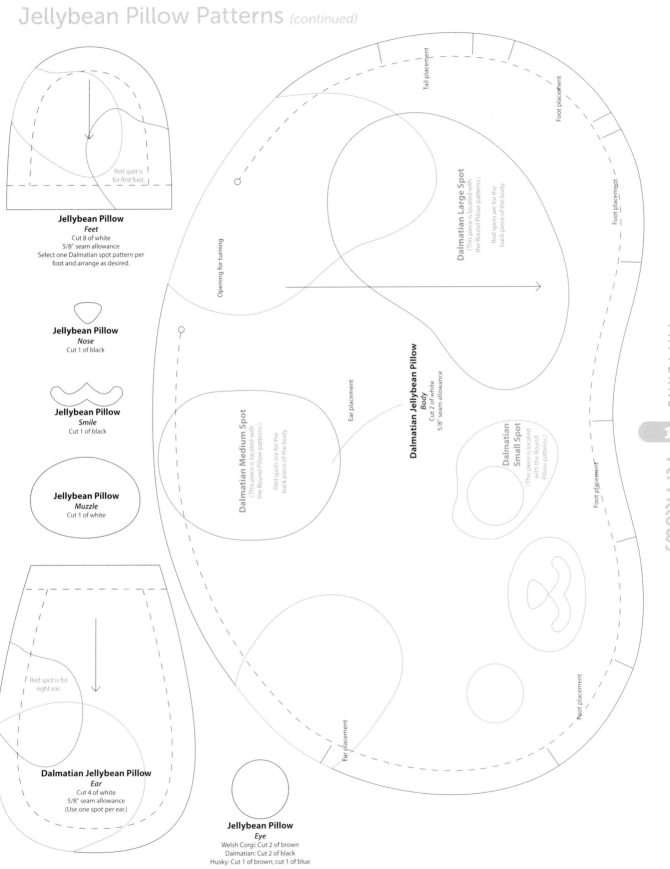

Jellybean Pillow
Feet
Cut 8 of white
5/8" seam allowance
Select one Dalmatian spot pattern per foot and arrange as desired.

Red spot is for first foot.

Jellybean Pillow
Nose
Cut 1 of black

Jellybean Pillow
Smile
Cut 1 of black

Jellybean Pillow
Muzzle
Cut 1 of white

Red spot is for right ear.

Dalmatian Jellybean Pillow
Ear
Cut 4 of white
5/8" seam allowance
(Use one spot per ear.)

Jellybean Pillow
Eye
Welsh Corgi: Cut 2 of brown
Dalmatian: Cut 2 of black
Husky: Cut 1 of brown, cut 1 of blue

Opening for turning

Tail placement

Foot placement

Foot placement

Dalmatian Large Spot
(This piece is located with the Round Pillow patterns.)
Red spots are for the back piece of the body.

Ear placement

Dalmatian Jellybean Pillow
Body
Cut 2 of white
5/8" seam allowance

Dalmatian Medium Spot
(This piece is located with the Round Pillow patterns.)
Red spots are for the back piece of the body.

Dalmatian Small Spot
(This piece is located with the Round Pillow patterns.)

Foot placement

Ear placement

Foot placement

Enlarge pattern 250% for actual size.

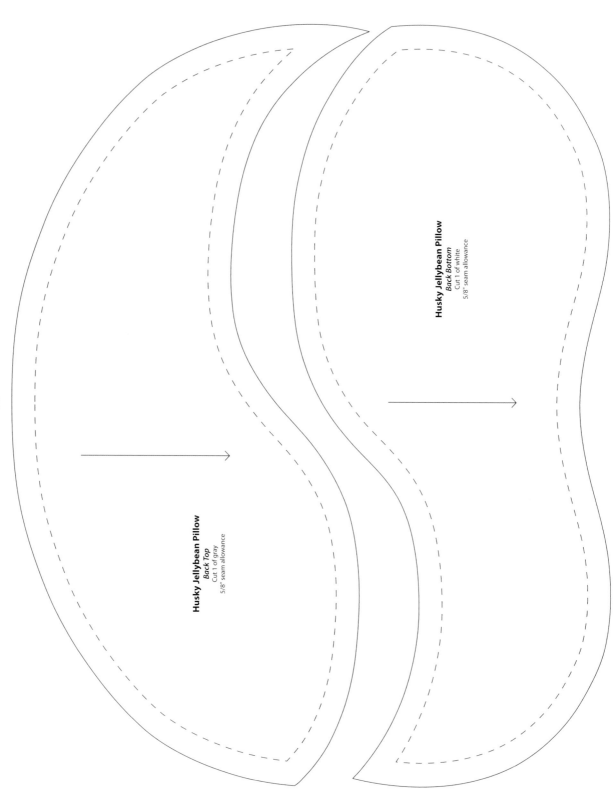

Husky Jellybean Pillow
Back Top
Cut 1 of gray
5/8" seam allowance

Husky Jellybean Pillow
Back Bottom
Cut 1 of white
5/8" seam allowance

Enlarge pattern 250% for actual size.

Jellybean Pillow Patterns *(continued)*

Husky Jellybean Pillow
Tail
Cut 2 of gray
5/8" seam allowance

Jellybean Pillow
Ear
Welsh Corgi: Cut 2 of brown, cut 2 of white
Husky: Cut 2 of gray, cut 2 of white
5/8" seam allowance
Select one Dalmatian spot pattern
per ear and arrange as desired.

Dalmatian Jellybean Pillow
Tail
Cut 2 of white
5/8" seam allowance
Select one Dalmatian spot pattern
and arrange as desired.

Round Pillow Patterns

Husky Round Pillow
Front Top
Cut 1 of gray on fold
5/8" seam allowance

Cut on fold

Husky Round Pillow
Front Bottom
Cut 1 of white on fold
5/8" seam allowance

Cut on fold

Round Pillow
Eye
Welsh Corgi: Cut 2 of brown
Dalmatian: Cut 2 of black
Husky: Cut 1 of brown, cut 1 of blue

Round Pillow
Muzzle
Cut 1 of white

Round Pillow
Nose
Cut 1 of black

Round Pillow
Smile
Cut 1 of black

Enlarge pattern 250% for actual size.

Round Pillow Patterns

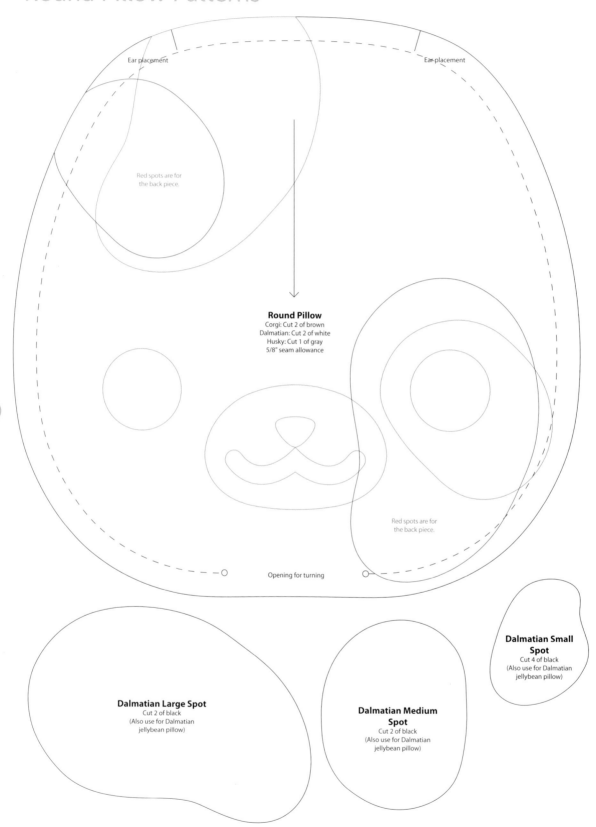

Ear placement

Ear placement

Red spots are for
the back piece.

Round Pillow
Corgi: Cut 2 of brown
Dalmatian: Cut 2 of white
Husky: Cut 1 of gray
5/8" seam allowance

Red spots are for
the back piece.

Opening for turning

Dalmatian Large Spot
Cut 2 of black
(Also use for Dalmatian
jellybean pillow)

**Dalmatian Medium
Spot**
Cut 2 of black
(Also use for Dalmatian
jellybean pillow)

**Dalmatian Small
Spot**
Cut 4 of black
(Also use for Dalmatian
jellybean pillow)

Enlarge pattern 250% for actual size.

Round Pillow Patterns *(continued)*

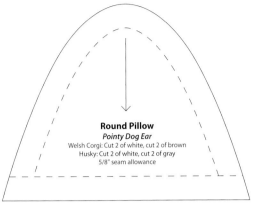

Round Pillow
Pointy Dog Ear
Welsh Corgi: Cut 2 of white, cut 2 of brown
Husky: Cut 2 of white, cut 2 of gray
5/8" seam allowance

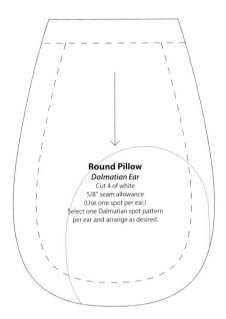

Round Pillow
Dalmatian Ear
Cut 4 of white
5/8" seam allowance
(Use one spot per ear.)
Select one Dalmatian spot pattern
per ear and arrange as desired.

Log Pillow Patterns

Opening for turning

Center top

Log Pillow
Body
Cut 1 on fold
5/8" seam allowance

Cut on fold

Center bottom

Enlarge pattern 250% for actual size.

Log Pillow Patterns *(continued)*

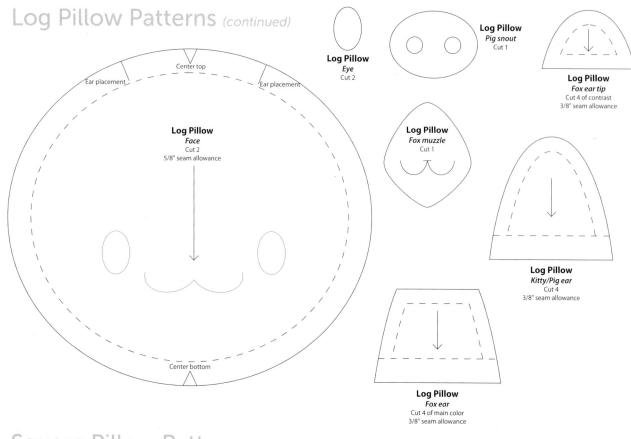

Log Pillow
Eye
Cut 2

Log Pillow
Pig snout
Cut 1

Log Pillow
Fox ear tip
Cut 4 of contrast
3/8" seam allowance

Log Pillow
Face
Cut 2
5/8" seam allowance

Center top

Ear placement

Ear placement

Center bottom

Log Pillow
Fox muzzle
Cut 1

Log Pillow
Kitty/Pig ear
Cut 4
3/8" seam allowance

Log Pillow
Fox ear
Cut 4 of main color
3/8" seam allowance

Square Pillow Patterns

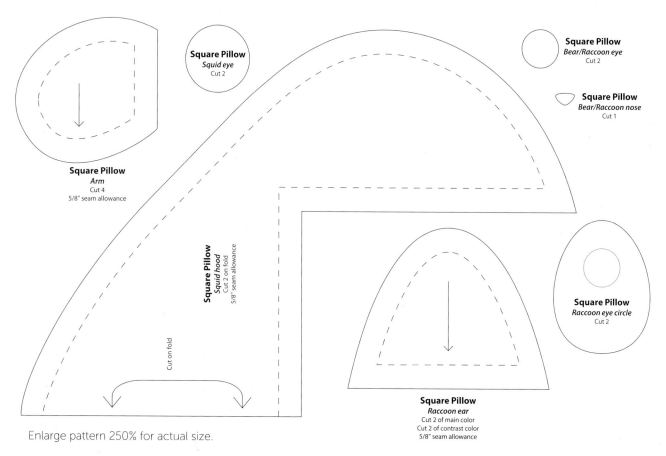

Square Pillow
Squid eye
Cut 2

Square Pillow
Bear/Raccoon eye
Cut 2

Square Pillow
Bear/Raccoon nose
Cut 1

Square Pillow
Arm
Cut 4
5/8" seam allowance

Square Pillow
Squid hood
Cut 2 on fold
5/8" seam allowance

Cut on fold

Square Pillow
Raccoon eye circle
Cut 2

Square Pillow
Raccoon ear
Cut 2 of main color
Cut 2 of contrast color
5/8" seam allowance

Enlarge pattern 250% for actual size.

PATTERNS

PET PILLOWS